BECOMING WEATHER

BECOMING WEATHER

POEMS

CHRIS MARTIN

COFFEE HOUSE PRESS
MINNEAPOLIS 2011

Coffee House Press books are available to the trade through our primary distributor, Consortium Book Sales & Distribution, www.cbsd.com or (800) 283-3572. For personal orders, catalogs, or other information, write to: info@coffeehousepress.org.

Coffee House Press is a nonprofit literary publishing house. Support from private foundations, corporate giving programs, government programs, and generous individuals helps make the publication of our books possible. We gratefully acknowledge their support in detail in the back of this book. To you and our many readers around the world, we send our thanks for your continuing support.

Good books are brewing at coffeehousepress.org

LIBRARY OF CONGRESS CATALOGING-IN-PUBLICATION DATA
Martin, Chris, 1977 Aug. 11–
Becoming weather / by Chris Martin.
p. cm.
ISBN 978-1-56689-259-9 (alk. paper)
I. Title.
PS3613.A77785B43 2011
811'.6-DC22
2010038009

Printed in the United States
3 5 7 9 8 6 4 2
FIRST EDITION

ACKNOWLEDGMENTS
Deep thanks to the following publications and their editors, where parts of *Becoming Weather* were allowed to bloom along the way: *A Public Space, Big Bell, Columbia Poetry Review, Forklift, Ohio, Fou, KGB Bar Lit, listenlight, Lungfull!, minor/american, Portable Boog Reader 3, Sixth Finch, Tight, Tool a Magazine,* and *VLAK.*

The title poem appeared as a broadside from Farfalla Press with art by George Schneeman.

The Small Dance was originally published as an e-chapbook through Scantily Clad Press.

Becoming Weather is especially indebted to the insight and commitment of Ted Mathys, Kendra Sullivan, Lisa Goldfarb, Stacy Pies, Greg Hewett, André Lepecki, Elaine Equi, and Mary Austin Speaker.

As always, the support of my family and friends has been invaluable, and I expect you will all find yourselves here.

Finally, I would like to embrace my extended family at Coffee House Press, past and present. I learned what I do with you and it feels good to come home.

BECOMING WEATHER

I keep trying to be honest in this glittering wind

— ALICE NOTLEY

Instability is necessary

— JOAN JONAS

DISEQUILIBRIUM

That the world is not striving toward a stable condition is the only thing that has been proved. Consequently one must conceive its climactic condition in such a way that it is not a condition of equilibrium—

— **FRIEDRICH NIETZSCHE**

I

Not that what

is is

not *actual,* these odd
bodies garbed in the accident

of space or, fantastic
autopsies, throbbing

as the moon is silent when you're not
looking at the beach

We, who may
fight as bravely for slavery
as for safety, the sun

crashing between train
cars like a drug
firing in the brain

And as that girl there
somnambulantly
drags a cord of hair

so it no

longer curtains her
shyly evading

eyes, elsewhere
a soldier steps across
the leaking resemblance of

a torso and a course

is determined to prolong

such images

2

One falls into all
the confusions of an equivocal
language, body moves

into itself, the eyes
disappear without

preparing for thought
which nonetheless

fills in—We perceive that
which exceeds us—A conflagration
of sapsuckers on the clothesline

Our arms grasping one
another's backs, stomachs bulging
to touch at the gnarled point

of their turning inward—Language
is a desert that holds us

all in unique
and inconceivable lateness

A crowd smoldering 'round
the skeleton of a two-headed calf
in a jar labeled *Spider*

The visitations of memory, busy
getting lost, recollect like clouds
whose hues trick us

into volume

3

Commuting through
Holland, 1945

on our way to *Dying*
Crapshooter's Blues

the long-forgotten
bulb shivers into a bloom

of eccentric shards
on the kitchen floor

I'm asking you
to accompany me

through the deformations
I'm asking you

if it's possible to refuse
to go blind—I for whom

the divers tones
of a mental life meld

at once
So is it

the infinite or
the instantaneous

quality of movement
that frightens us more?

Do verbs only betray
the impossibility of not acting?

Let's say I was looking
into the absence

where my face would be
Let's say I found

my whole body's thought

4

So much in my life happens
that's not poetry

these days—the drugged-out
glare of the boy embarrassed by

his grasp of fractions and yet
his laughter is impressive

The kangaroos in the park
that lean suspiciously
on their tails bleed into the heart

of a mouse stretched like a ribbon
across the curb—Certain

small mysteries continue
to animate the instant—This morning

I dreamt I was purchased
by reclusive Italian merchants

to fix their youngest daughter
who spoke only in tongues

and woke to the hydraulics
of the bus picking up

a flock of strangers
outside the movie theater—There
is nothing arbitrary about this

5

To be blind each day
is a senseless response

The wall outside the train
window reads POCKET

POOL CHAMP as the hollow
of my silent cheek forms

its own rank pouch
I was so sure I could go

hours without taking a breath
that I forgot to learn how

it is that breath takes me

6

What we ask ourselves
now is—*What is
forgivable?*

I move to bare
the little splitting
inside as it

reds between
the pink on the end
of my finger

Somehow this coincides
with a faith in
the world as a place

to go on
living

We wake in a catastrophe and move
about the city in a tiny
raft of glee, my gaze always

already yellow because I'm not severe
like a dancer, nor perverse
like Balthus, though of course

I am
both

7

Not to harass nor harness
the world with the eye's
promiscuities I think

I am a thoroughfare
where various energies
transact and curve

so to lose love is to have
a dire portion of oneself
attenuated and totter

the streets both freezing
and overheated, blank
as a plank of wood, to go

out slurring over
the resemblances

8

Can I say the air
is beautiful?

Can I spend my whole life
as a guest inside the eccentric
balloon?

Let us release
these appearances
and in so

doing hold
fast to what burden
bodies make

thick returning
to us their
unconscious care

Can I spend my whole life as a gust
outside the eccentric balloon?

Can I see the air
as beautiful?

9

What is a favorite number
except a protection
against weather?

This is my favorite number
because I was sick
of getting older—Is it so

common then to become
weary over the worry
of glut, the way it brazenly

shifts into need?

I do laundry
get a haircut
make coffee
pet the cat

and obtain an active sort

of boredom—It is abhorrent
to me to know
beforehand what a thing is

to become

The unconscious
is not incautious

I could have said *the silence*
of Marcel Duchamp is overrated

I could say *the forms*
of farms are far from exhausted

but instead trudge lips
pursed as the leather suitcases
in the tunnel on
the way to the 4 train bob

moronic like birds

and a transient
serenades himself with Sam
Cooke in the keyed
gleam of an advertisement

for a European-produced compact
disc promising NOW!
as if the satori of hundreds
of bodies rushing together

wasn't enough

II

A word is to me

like a button

potentializing

a handful of noise

(let me say it more directly)

A word is to me

various and becoming

(no, more directly)

A word is to me

toward

The light rough
The sunshine unsure

The skin of things
pushing at the hinge
of the eye

as an unin-
terruptedness

wrests disclosure into song

I start to melt without
startle without tumult

Like Muddy
Waters strangling
the very air

I'm a man

becoming weather

13

I can only begin
this once
I know enough not
to begin again

Bus engines rev the avenue
to remind me of time's
masculine passing

The people I love
lack something sufficient
for the violence of this world

If you recognize the flower's use
as a Geiger counter

you no longer look
down upon its mute beauty

14

Now   if you would

gently   tip

the assemblage

I will breathe

my torrent

once more

15

Do I suffer only
from abundance?

I watch our sun
play against the bodega
glass and across

the face of an ad
that reads *Witches
in Bikinis!*

When I ate Alex's last
balled-up one-dollar
bill, I was somewhat
ill for several days

The bum in the bookstore
is fast asleep in the poetry

aisle, his chest
ballooning against
the titles, while outside

the MTA strikes
and at home the wailing
of molecular discordances
is drowned out by

the whistle of the radiator or
the hum of the desktop or
the strings of the guitar

which confide certain melodies
before they even strike

the eye's wet edge

16

If refuse is the refuge of time

If philosophy is music with content

If our singing only serves
to reveal the impossible

I still want to be real
as a hamburger

Ordering coffee at noon
under doused neon

the girl behind
the counter exposes

the match-sized gap
between her incisors

Teeth are said to erupt

A man is said to live by his tooth

Given particular cadences
of joy my mouth
spills open like a fortune cookie

17

A part of the scorpion feeds
us indefensible ideas

The panopticon falls apart
when sufficiently fingered

When Marina becomes a part of

the gun she is not
the one that stops
the performance

Living still, as
we do, amid

the immediacies
of lack and glut

(however)

The windows look both
into and onto

as our voices transmute
the blank room

sepulchral, wintery
light to camera

lucida, tobacco-tinged
fingers to morning's bacon

(nonetheless)

When the voices reverse
into snaps the steam

that ascends 54th Street
on the arthritic stems

of undressed city trees
pleases us greatly

for having made
them burlesque again

A painted shadow
does not change

A legion of secrets

to equivocate
to avoid

the mistake of closure

War nods off
but keeps a spare
eye always open

The weather's gentle

glossolalia

Paper over shoulder
reads *meet triplets*
with identical boob-jobs!

20

If, like
electrons, we

move fast enough
in unforseen

directions, will
we finally

appear or
disappear?

One must be very humane
to say *I don't know that*

So is it indolence to speak
in the words of others

in mere purchases, rehearsals?
For instance, are we allowed

to imagine Adam as a child?
In the dream the spirit

of my grandfather
entered me and called

itself *a current*
of fortuitous noise

22

(birdsong)

I am not speaking
of the song of

(eyesong)

existence, I am
singing song

(amsong)

is existence

23

I wanted a kind
of wildness

pivots of unpredictability
went my whole

life without seeing
a lick of land

(*the fat yogurt moon*)

So my father and I sawed
boards and painted them black
to fashion a bat's house

and when the bat died we shook
him out and broke the wood
to dissipate the coffin

(*the black soda moon*)

or earlier we filled our tube
socks with dirt, tied
the color-ringed ends together

and flung them between the midnight
pines for a sonar–trained tooth

to catch, to clutch, but not
to let the bat go

(*the drug dreg moon*)

24

It's Saturday at the park
bulldogs whining at the clop

of horses, muscles curdling
Napoleon's trusty Marengo

preserved minus his left hoof
which was duly fashioned

into a snuffbox for some rich fucker
and his yellow-faced progeny

Robert Wadlow was someone
I loved as a child—Made of his corpus

a secret beneath several tons
of truckloaded cement—The sun forgets

us and fragile
illuminations from my lamp
appear in the window
across the street

Thus I steal
with relaxed muscles

allowing each miniscule parcel
to pierce me with its thrill

25

When the Catfish
is in Bloom

the afternoon
drags saturnine

sunlight mouthing
tones into a leafless

tree, winter's
improvisation

voiced by ice, the air
meeting itself in arabesques

and myself asking
what would it be
not to teem?

We finger
the corporeal fret

beneath our words, let one
voice slide only to lift

at the reticular
convergence
of others

26

Before I hear it, I experience
the lull before
the kettle's whistle, even

over the lower
hiss of the radiator

Apartments are full
of snakes and birds that turn

out to be tea on the way

lull
guess
kettle
hiss
full

Lorraine says *February
is expanding*

The ad says *You may
experience faintness*

Understanding has everything
to do with dance's
instability, the stuttering way one

brings on
brings in
brings forth

repetition

27

It was the night of the executed coat
thief's dismemberment, the night

we realized a knife
is a pen when it's
inside the body

You asked me to conspire
against the trap
of the corpse

A convergence

of grieving bodies
within the body
of a makeshift box

A gift of the hand to the hand

of another out
of a love of giving

(pirouette)

I thought
to people

the poem
to a ripping

point only
to find it

taut again

Cabin arid

Oakland to Brooklyn
with bodies that
insist, persist, insist

The woman once
asleep in her light
green shirt startles

into seeing, tenebrous
light on my lap
arriving in pulses

from the tip of the wing

Life is not so far
as the tip
of one's nose

Descent iridescent

30

(today)

They removed the Psychic
sign from the eave

but underneath the bum
is still hunting

bag / huff / laugh / bob

(many months previous)

So many men
named Hans

were limping
in the marathon

I was crying
I always cry

at marathons

(death)

We feel greener as pain
dutifully circulates

futile little
flowers bend

interiorly

(tomorrow)

31

An affinity for visions

implicates a structure

of permeability

How then does
one put it

aside?

I was listening
to *Jesus, etc.*

the apartment on
the first floor was looted

the Pistons were beating
the Cavaliers and a helicopter

crashed in the Afghani desert
so more Americans

could die estranged

The earth only receives
a tenth of one percent

of the sun's
radiated energy

You were right about the stars

They're just like us

32

I woke from a nap to the image
of a woman I had loved

naked on a couch, her hair
touching her breasts, a lightning

storm over Quepos

What would it mean
for this to be a secret?

My heart's been one beat
too loud every
four, its effusive

knock troubling, the used-car
balloon gorilla trembling
its back to me through the window

of the F train over
the Gowanus Canal

I want to negotiate
the obtuseness
of winter, am left lusty

listening for spring

And when it returns
we will not so much

be relieved
as relived

33

When the lovers were out
of focus they multiplied

34

Soon it will be April
and someone turned on
all the birds

35

We ended up
on the Westside

Highway covered
in Drambuie

I had no idea
how sticky it was

In the morning
coffee on my nose

swooshing across
Broadway to talk

a phenomenology
of nuclear hands

mine shaking
the man asking

what it is a body *does*?

36

(April 3)

Not often is it that I grace
my own eyes

which tend to tend to
more removed entities or
look out at some middle

distance in a great green
float of thought

(April 4)

On street my eyes caught
glance of man

cradling shattered hand
and found myself

trailing a discrete
line of his blood
five or six blocks

to where it mutely stopped

(April 5)

Look out the window—fix
your eyes on
one thing—attend

to the words that flutter
around it—now
think about the poem

we have all been
writing

37

If I possess only distances
this is only true in that

it is accurate—If poetry is nothing
more than arithmetic

and proof, there remains
no way of separating me

from an economy
of me: blue
jeans, sweat beads
a knuckle airily

popping, record
player broken, the flitting
exigencies of song

arbitrarily carried by the street below

The mugs in the cupboard
shudder as a train
passes, the shifting limit

of equilibrium ceaselessly
lurching askew

I ask you to devise a monstrance
to bear necessary questions

I ask you to think of the soldier
as a prosthesis

I ask you to remember the ending
of *Cobra Verde,* how Kinski finally collapsed

and the deformed man quit
his pursuit to gaze upon it

These surprises return us
to the galaxy named *Fangs*

A scorpion
A panopticon

I ask you to prepare an aperture
I ask you to take my hand

I ask you (whispering)
which is the way

that leads
me to you?

A SHORT HISTORY OF ORDER

First there was no first, but only a middle. The first act against the body was to fashion a first. First there were animals and man among them. Then there was man and animals among him. He walked upright and discovered the number *one*. He walked upright and counted his possessions. The body was no longer long, but vertical—a point interrogating the landscape. Then tools to extend the body, to give it prosthesis, to kill and defend from a distance. But the world remained too near. So it was that we doubled the world and then chose its double. So it was that the shadow became the thing and the body a shadow cast by the mind. And the body became its double. And the body found itself in a mirror. And the body became a page, and the page became a pixel, and the pixel became a volumeless potential. And the body disappeared because it was always moving. Ambiguous bodies were obliterated, indeterminate matter was destroyed. And the we we were not became the we we were. It was the projection, the screen, the surface uncoupled from its mass. Just as gold became paper and paper became plastic and plastic became nothing. The body unhinged itself from itself, leaving its mass behind like a snake-spirit. In order to slough the body, we gave it to the animals. And it only returned to us in animal moments. In bloodshed and birth. The body only returned when it broke. And even then we did not recognize it. The body was flayed and became words. The body was weighed and became money. And money, like language, is for burning. So no one was surprised when the body went up in smoke.

THE SMALL DANCE

In the midst of standing still something else is occurring and the name for that is the small dance.

— STEVE PAXTON

I

Societies of superfluity
require doses   of the end

     of the world

It was Wednesday morning
we were exploring

     a poetry of a dancer to dance a haircut
so it is already happening—one takes
     the first step in a dance away

from transcendence and is now
     an infinite

     distance removed

I wake thinking

              atrocious, atrocious

      horses moving diagonal

        in the shadow

             of a plane

Now the tragedy is anatomical   except
I'm no longer good

at transducing tragedy   instead

             go hungry waiting
             for others in a country

where only

    images like torsos

               arriving from the sea arrive

    and linger like the cat   in the backyard

             nursing alertly

3

Do you explain

           ice by acting

    slippery?

Simply   by moving we implicate   the hoax

     of time so it

is already   changing

        a pull in the lapse

   a voice to recover

           the present

           covert even

     from ourselves

4

Today is wrought by a lingering
thingishnessless
                              a planet that desires

          what it dooms into orbit

                    Today the trees
                              are fraught with gossip

          about being and the selves

                                        who we are
                    are moving
                                        targets
It's said one's either
poet or assassin
                    but we've grown

          conspiratorial   being both

5

I would like to   be able to   describe to

     you a stillness

but yawning   at the funeral
          was a kind of dance   these flags
    refolding
         another

     In Japan god

        stands on an artichoke
     but here in America

we take the PATH train to Journal Square and the first
    store we see boasts
        99¢ DREAMS

     One wakes only
           to this false peace
   with the voice
       of a weatherman

6

Then having forgone the rectangle
of tamed light for a structure that is itself
               rhythm   hymn-like

    our voices were overlaid
    in a dizzying charge   I got lonely

thinking about how the galaxies are
         so big they run

right into one another and never
                      even touch
    Then I got self-interrogatory

             with caustic shifts
    sticky fingers

    and disappearing blips   afraid
        the dead will see

        I'm not very brave
        or worse that
               I am

7

The vowels are valves

        The song is an answer

And this is a question

           of forces

      a voice   to recover

from ourselves

      a step   to take

   back from the edge's smirking

   lip and toward the collected works

of Gottfried Wilhelm Leibniz

8

It is no   accident the philosopher

comes to himself by being thrown to the ground

          as apparently berserk we
                    continue to sweep the bodies

          into the future   conjuring awe

                    on the outskirts of war

even our bones grown only

                    to be ravaged
          each cicada
                              The middle is not

average   it's where things pick up

                    speed

9

I'm still recovering
                              from the tingle
              of the hairdresser's razor
                        on the triangle

           of Broadway to work to
                         my one-way street, Brooklyn
                   the way one step
                                    insinuates its
                        others endlessly

I have found myself suffused
                                       by rough light

              unexpectedly pierced to haunt

When the poet pictures   someone jerking

         off on   a marble

         statue, off-white on
         off-white, we   finally see how

              dance is born

                   from abundance

10

        The other me in my
dream said shed

                                the semiotic for
        the seismic

and since wind has   proved presence

to be a form

                        of magnetism

        the leaves do not need   to learn how

to tremble   though

                                probably the world is too
sure about its things

II

                To truly understand
    one

                must nest

                            subcutaneous
        bed beneath
                            the counterfeit

                            of architecture
and attend
                        each dislocation
                                        of grace

        When one sparrow veers the whole   flock warps

    into rearrangement

                    Peril is just   another

                    word   for body

Cop choppers
                    above Windsor
Terrace where
                    below the squeal

                              of the train's brakes
        rang to a stop

The USPS worker riding the F was reading

                    Danielle Steele past a thick gold chain

The toddlers played T-ball   between the brownstones

But if I say   the fixture   of the man

that sits   huffing glue beneath the Psychic's eave

                    clutches a crumpled brown paper

bag to his heart   can this here still

        be a nature poem?

To say blood   is the medium is

also to say blood   is the middle

a location that   spills continually

into itself   To say breath

is the medium is   also to say breath

is the middle   a locution

that spells what   is continually

given   To say song

is the medium   is also to say

song is the middle's   allocation

of universe that needs   to hear itself

We disclose so much   simply

by beginning   again

14

We awe even
at the airport
terminal's chaotic banality
a vast array of
human hives
to shore against
lack as the chorus
intensifies
Quite often it is
the coincidence   crashing
quiet quiet
crash
a form of heat lightning perhaps

an invisible excess   from above so

I never learned to separate
people from principles

So what

A cauterizing horse escapes the hood
          of some rich fucker's car while night
      gradually curves like a vowel

    Last night the word   appeared to

me in a dream—SUNGHOST—but receiving no
        directions on how to
                   split it it
    remained hinged   another thing
                to traverse
This afternoon I looked
        skyward at the sound
         of a helicopter only

    to find a caterpillar
      wriggling midair

A fascination with the rearrangement
     of animals
             A sleepy love with racing breasts
        An avenue to turn paralysis
That which
            remains part of the fiction remains
     New York
               glass shards
         in the grass
      helicopters
                a situation we can't
     stop immaculating   each one of us veering

           into the joke
as likewise I tear
at *Red Shift*
         blooming beard and ride the train's

    lurch and return I   always knew the reason

      there was no reason   fit

I stopped not   looking and got   stuck that way

He dreams *lovely* allows

                           him into the afterworld

Sunlight goads again

               so I am

      unbalancing   like an echo

       from the known history of dance

and the train car

      in the photograph reads *Pussy*

                    is God as

the restless murmur
of metallic things   continues

         so I promise to never   stop moving
I promise
        to always go

             sincere in the blur

A whole system of gravitational muscles, whose action for the most part eludes conscious attention and will, is responsible for assuring our posture: these muscles maintain our equilibrium and permit us to stand without having to think about it. It so happens that these muscles are also those which register the changes in our affective and emotional state. Thus, every modification of our posture will intersect with our emotional state, and reciprocally, every affective charge will bring with it a modification, however imperceptible, in our posture.

— HUBERT GODARD

In the same way

                  music disturbs

     a silence

               that never was

We find parts

     of ourselves torn into

            frays of sonic excess

and others snarled in the convolutions

            of an always already

        choreographed world

I do a small dance only   to find it

                  enormous

     do a so

        simple step to end

     up staggering in

           fury

20

The poor own the clouds
and we love them for it

I was out interviewing clouds   amassing
the notes of a sky pornographer   while patches

of the city subnormalized
by fear of fear   like a reef bleaching closed

I took to the streets
looking for a human velocity

feeling   disequilibrium

heavy in the abundance
of summer light
the silent apathy
of stars   which is neither
silent nor apathetic
I   am   becoming   weather
and
I don't
plan on doing
it alone

22

Most stay testing   the gray
        balloon brains of their
                                enemies
            we swell
                It's Sunday   a cat erupts

on the nightstand and wine
                moves into the socks

        Spent the afternoon ogling
        mugshots at the precinct

            so many torn
                            out eyes
There was a movie on TV

about dudes   blowing other dudes

        apart

            Outside a quick quivering bird took
            refuge in a length of pipe
                            Being a thing it bursts
                into events

Sure I was a molecule

                                  accumulating talk

    I came to this wanting

                                to say something

              small about being

     with you

                       an awkwardness beneath gasoline

          each weird hospitality flung

              into the mouth of a passing bird

We woke refurbishing the war   a rabbit that blooms

     in my ears   the man loves art because

         he is an egoist   in my ears   he is an egoist

Today is something thrown and awaiting

                              purchase

The rappers say   *it's like that*

and ask   *can I live?*

This is insect speed and we

           must be legendary in our hush

    corpuses thrumming open

              as a patina of grief

        corrodes unnoticed in a background

          of yesterday's teeth

        as the newspaper reads *tiny coffin moves*

scientists to tears

          our extravagances gather

This is deep speed or a dynamism

        of the middle   prone

            to disappearance

    A speed slowed past capital

          in the slick of the thing music

There is still nothing

        like looking at the swimming

    pools of America through

           our airplane windows

        the clouds caught heavy

as doubt against

         the apparent

           curvature of the sky

     I am so not

         thinking these days

    I am so wavelets

           We went to bed early after

   screwing by

        the light of the KEY FOODS

27

No one seeks peril and yet
there it is   there is

peril in admiring the trees

28

By entering this   dense dance
    I do not mean to
       revert to a dazzling   dumb-mobile

The wind warps my breath   the air errs and the pivot

      of my crash moves on   pilotless

           The hives, which were people
      Death, which is a question

    The love that leaves me   too turned

      on to write   the woods
       in the city teeming   with words

that rustle and stumble
      other vectors catching on
   unevenness
        Only lies slide
              so I felt the necessity
     for a chorus

The flowers   the flowers   what
                                     would it mean to be a bee?
to speak in swerves in
                         a force voice?
                                                Words
           make things name
                                        One tongue travels near
                                  the other and the whole
picture unravels
                              into movement   this
is not love but it might
                                dance
                                       or other synonymous
states
            paronomasia and miasma
                  shaking the entirety in turn
                                                tuning flux
and flaring   at the imperceptible

                                  fringes of collision
To say the dancer doesn't think   while dancing is
         to say we still haven't thought   what it is
                                  a body does

TOWARD CORPOREAL ORDER

Until one day the question was asked: how can we speak in the common language that binds us of the things that that bond obliterates? And we began to look for answers. And we realized looking was part of the difficulty. So we began saying yes less to our eyes and began instead with the laying on of hands. But that wasn't enough. What we needed was born in coincidence, where the muddle of the middle becomes thick with information. So we learned to heap and leap in the plenum, learned to return synesthetic, all sense grown immense in its overlap. And the answers began amid the movement of these moments. The body, in moving, removed so much unnecessary thought. The straight lines fell away, the geometry and frames. Curves surged into place, the vacuity of space flooded and fled. In this abundance, this dance of answers, one answer was the form from which the others emerged. This answer, of course, was the body. And the body, of course, is full of answers. We called it corporeal order: that which speaks volume in overspill, excess, slip, and surprise; that which will not be still. We learned perpetual rearrangement, learned to stray from the dictates of convenience. We looked without carving, saw without severing. And it was difficult. And it required both colossal and minute attention. And it involved loving no while nurturing a deep and protracted yes. And it has been years since we first heard ourselves speak it and it will be years yet before the intolerable secret it has become our duty to reveal is fully disclosed.

THIS FALSE PEACE

I was just looking for a moment of peace,
but it made me feel murderous.

— ELAINE EQUI

There is such action here   the yard we can't decide   is front

or back   black fly chasing   my breath   sister tentative

on harmonica   over leaves' dip and twist   frantically modern

though their shadows show   them up   as bees are likewise

out-ghosted by a hummingbird   already gone   and neither

of us feels the least bit   ironic about it   living amid

machines   of thought   whose blown geometries   forge

the sleeplessness of unnamable desires   paying our ears

to the simple ridiculous happinesses   a plane blanketing air's

blank   to scissor through   aghast at the plural   interloping

so overlapping tones   to startle at the jackhammer's bony

knock   to woodpecker   to want these things to *thing*   for us

we want   to see so as only   to settle   into a blinding

It was Saturday   cicadas   our expiring   mechanisms hidden

in the leaves   I was thinking about literalness   or the case

of nerves   a body seemed to be   jettisoned   for more

aqueous matter   a wave that always   crashing never

crashes   a color the current   world opening and charge

to loiter among flowers   devoid   of the kind of

frictionlessness particular   to capitalism   or was it just

heat lightning   over the territories   a litter of cats

skittish in back   the air-conditioner's sound   a skin

canceling crickets   oh frenzy   convenience   the honey

in my coffee   resolutely aloof   a leaf is a symptom of excess

the world opening unto want   nerves   waves   honey

Everything insists   on reappearing or   it's a silly conceit

that leaves need   attendance   that the omnipresent

cable wires winding black   like severed vines from off

the brick is only artful   in the frame   of some manly attention

ceiling fan in burble   rabbit ears' awkward jut   a fly that

scampers frenzied beneath   the lampshade and the phone

is silent   or   fruition   the phone if Heidegger's

is obscene   obscuring what normal   morality   the ear

insists that leaves   need   a backyard   or cable wires

buffeting brick   is only artful   the ceiling   fan framing

the fly   scampers frenzied or is   silent is   obsolete

An immense   rain and nothing was saluting   nobody

at home it was the fear   I would become   knock-kneed

but that was the year I learned   to fear war   more

and thought disfigurement   an easily paid   retainer

hidden orthotics in the closet   amid Christmas lights

at school the substitute   regaled us   gruesomely

how his friend's brains   invaded his face   the painstaking

way they were removed   from his ear   the night

we first bombed Iraq I was older   thought my orthotic

trick stupid   had just returned from learning   the myriad

ways one   might die   underwater   though the rain

stopped the news   kept pouring in   my knees were fine

It's afternoon and I look   ragged like   a flower weapon
begging seed   I can't stop desiring   sidereality
that tremors the air   with its dislocations   of course I'm afraid
of women   I'm afraid of men too   the day thrown   to bits
symphonic   goading   a word like cognac   to buffet the skull
a cognate lurking insidious   like country air   in the real
estate office   or a cephalopod   changing hue   the world
persists   machinic   hackneyed   ragged and I want you
to find the little strip   or incommensurate weft   I want
to bed   in the unknowing   our fingers become   air   light
catastrophe   you don't understand   I *care* about the movies

Joan of Arc's biography   with Biggie on car   stereo outside

the trees compulsively   shedding buds   that form a pattern

around the fire   hydrants   it's less   the arch   of a story

than the fact that   there are only situations   since thirty

years have not brought me   closer to seeing   past the gossip

of being   its small   talk rumoring the air   the sunlight

redacted   giving only   the heaviness of rage   a mouth

a word like hydrant   or dehydrated   maybe dromedary

the ligaments sewn   with light unconsciously pervading

the wound always   slightly open   it's less   that I see

through my face than that   the world looks   toward

I am not the one   thinks the disordered part   disorders

the whole   am I?   reggae punctuating   street or birdsong

the helicopter deeply   then ambulances   mediating joy

a Braille of slumping shadows   that ride away   like desire's

desire to be more   or less   desired   a friction engine

charging asymmetrical   the song asks who   you gonna ride

with boy?   I'm gonna slit the gray balloon   brains of my great

enemy and breed   sulfur in a flummoxing   smog   train

it to believe   in the shapes the sleepers   make breathing

where there   is only this death   we die not   dying

in a song   made of detours   god   is what we make of

It is said that the last   woman who tattoos   you is your wife

a sudden self   or cipher   interpellated   by faces

the birds here   tattoos that move   over speech   a man's

expensive   shoes invade me   ballistic earrings   quiver

'round the soft circle of a neck   this is our pantomime of not

falling   the way peace   attenuates   and distends

into war's perpetual   rebound   this is our effort   to relocate

no stillness   the small dance   whose caught   topography

covers the street   with torture so   plain it seeps into garlands

even   islands of nail   clippings ripping the leaves   all

matter   inebriated   tenebrous   boomeranging   wet

we awed so much   that tending to   life put us to sleep

I can't stop sensing   movieness   black braids grazing

the outstretched   wings of the television   antenna frozen stoic

a mathematics of hate   intuitive   or else   we have

become its harvester   the blink accident   blink waves   once

I thought distance euphoric   now I find its lie   most common

a vast and incurious thing   to put holes in people   put holes

in a tiny black   braid that moves   through air   the air

the air   which is so   smug sometimes   but can I say it

is beautiful?   the soft   hollow of a gut   dribbling

words are not secrets   words are not secret   yes they are

Atmosphere concerning   a version   of blank we sweat

to dissipate the sure   empire of knowledge   these daily

nuptials   braiding air to bone or   lost here   the television's

nuclear   I want to kiss you   as the phone   rings but you

are the one   calling   punching voices   into strip   or

braiding the ends   to rejoice   in the already   in that

we punctuated   the sky with lack   manning our nation's

boredom   plus shrieks of conscience   getting drunk keeps

happening   in words   stars' shapely   tricking us into flight

all our dicks in a row   cornering   the brain   which was itself

perseverating   or perverse for   a version of blank

I wanted to leave   a testament to the real   to things

verily happening   above truth   punching voices

to always go   sincere   to always   go sincere in the blur

so if it   is already happening   it is already changing

beneath vast shadows   of dulled drunkards   in uneasy amaze

people are more   interesting than poems   but we need them

to understand them   terror is only another   kind of error

there is too much   choice but there is never enough

choosing   a flock that   perforates the sky   into arrows

but what is an arrow   if it is   always moving?   this

is a year   in the life   of going   to the movies   is there

a part of me that is a part   of history?   It is unimportant

The first   day in October and how   I burden the apartment

with sneezes   lemons from the bodega exploding   with seed

a pagoda on the edge of   the lake in flames   my nose

still running   once I had an earthquake   in my ears   it is

the first   with sneezes   how I burden   these earthquakes

into whisper-talk   to make our caricature   of air   we call it

on the off   chance   a finish   that chokes what it makes

shine   I did not want the abstraction of being   out for a walk

she lied   when she swore she   wouldn't read the moon any

longer   no small assailant   of mirror-light   in my ears

October talk   the hyphen's edge   then I is heterogeneous

for being electric   abstraction like circles   for the moon

Don't use words   Don't use words   Don't use words

Getting drunk keeps   cornering the brain   and in that we
punctuated happening   but you're the one saved   intelligence
never wanting Wednesday   to end   or the abstraction of being
separate   time tolls   I sneeze   the neighbors name
their dog   Silence   take it out   for a walk   to wonder
what air might confide   incipience   a flooding   that adds
imperceptibly to each   wrenching turn   the surface a glue
to terrify   or god   keeps happening   this inundation
to harbor time's sneeze   in the flood   I want to sleep in
the sleep you   sleep as ferociously one   must drive on
to tenderness   repetition is desire   a sneezing sun that gropes
dark stiletto   branches   Silence is what insists   on noise

Neptune is in tatters   the way   the shreds of the eye project

the room   of our mooring and if   our false light   stutters

neon neon none   this false peace reads   witness witless white

except it's now   become not "life"   but a slow explosion

all flesh become sound become   a light   sound as in   *flash*

of course it is   color   this mooring   material   this naked

darkness just now   perforated by Guston's pinkening   red

a wartime   color for lovers   whose hands could not stop

traveling   to stub   at rough light   dire light   light of the

haptic   awake   even war murmuring   of   of   *of*

Morning   mooring   murmuring   this is a room

for incipient conspiracies   bulbs   separated by strangulations

the whirling grace   of a world not yet   gone   sharp

as *Poor Boy Long*   *Ways from Home* plays   adjacent

do the walls need   contempt?   can I manage to escape

the deep double-jointedness of women?   I want to sleep in

the repetitions   of desire   order only   another

Jack and ginger   while the birds of New Mexico play ghost

to our ears   so how come the girl   at the bar   glinted?

I ended   up smoking with my feet   out the window

questioning   the fetishistic appearance of pure objectivity

perhaps I was made to   ruin it   to sleep in   the ear's

dislocation and return   to the middle   perforated by grace

The shadows tease   us with what we   come to be
simultaneity   of depthlessness   floored   by Agnes'
tiny nimrod machines   punctuating death   discretely   as if
the mess of bodies   could   thrill rhythm   as if the mass
were less   flesh more dry   and still   my face feels full
of contingencies   for I am not   a quick-enough politician
as if man was doomed   to *man*   though clearly the light
is mostly *igh*   and in this we   found ourselves refuting awe
our bones growing translucent   skin   like a dapper cape or
paper cup   then again I think   *igh*   is mostly I

Sleep is a story   we tell ourselves   the streets yellow

with swollen leaves   your face   somewhere in mine

orange   gone suddenly   sensual   in what you called

the inequality   of silences   the air now thirsty   even

our naps   grown cinematographic   itching joy   lugging

flowers   into the future   without a map   everyone

suddenly so New   Wave looking   at you from the bar

jukebox's already   alone grin   flush   a closed explosion

took the top   off   as only yesterday   I was so

sure silence   didn't exist   now   bursting

Sure I came to   speak of sound's   perplexing   glee

there were   dead animals speaking   through our fingers

like glue   each sunset like   the poverty   of staring

at newsstands   I have loved you without   having to

write   a givenness given   freely and without   light

that's why all these new mothers won't stop   looking at me

or is it because Isaac Newton died   a virgin   no wonder

everyone thinks the planets   remain   apart   to have loved

without   resorting   to gravity to   touch that which touches

though the color   from our bodies still began   its journey

to burned-out stars   the sunset   perplexing   literal   a breath

that rides   sound's dizzy   all these voices   perseverating

This is not just   a love letter   it is one fragment of
the treatise on   reversibility   the way   this glove touches
the hand touching   you   some call it looking at the moon
through the word   when it first happened   I was as far from
myself as air is   from the periodic table   my ears
hearing *I* and then   *if* but it   was and would always
be *of*   this is not a desire   for order   this is that which
is in continual   reprisal   just as weather is   surely
the first of all   arts   the first of all   artists   you are here
amid   as umbilical illuminations   fill the cloud body

CODA

BEING OF

Of course there

are answers

in the trees, why else

would they be

there? The shapes are

answers, color

is an answer, a hummingbird

makes an answer of

noise, speed, glass

answers slowly, the air

is a reminder

of an answer said so

early that it needs

to be repeated

now and now

again, the leaves

answer with green applause

the spaces say

please and that is also

an answer, I try

so hard to exact

things and am so densely

removed

from them, but every once

in a while I see fit

to absorb a weightless

answer, an answer without

volume, because

light is there! And all of

the sudden I am

perforated with it

and give off a small

answer of

my own, but let's

not be content

with that, let's touch each

other and go on

stupid and wait without

the sense of it

so soon

enough we can return to

our entanglements, if

only to return from there

to air, to

being of.

THE CHORUS

David Abram

Henri Bergson

Edmund Berrigan

Ted Berrigan

Joseph Beuys

Joshua Clover

Andrew Conn

Robert Creeley

Guy Debord

Gilles Deleuze

Jacques Derrida

Jean Epstein

John Fahey

Hubert Godard

Elizabeth Grosz

Felix Guattari

Barbara Guest

Stephen Heath

Martin Heidegger

Lyn Hejinian

Daniel Heller-Roazen

Greg Hewett

Jill Johnston

Erica Kaufman

Julia Kristeva

Jeff Mangum

Maurice Merleau-Ponty

Eileen Myles

Friedrich Nietzsche

Will Oldham

George Oppen

Rainer Maria Rilke

Sean Simon

Jack Spicer

Benedictus Spinoza

Kendra Sullivan

Jeff Tweedy

Paul Valéry

Virginia Woolf

C. D. Wright

CHRIS MARTIN is the author of *American Music*, selected by C. D. Wright for the Hayden Carruth Award, and was named one of the Poetry Society of America's New American Poets in 2010. He cofounded and edited the online magazine *Puppy Flowers* for its entire ten-year run and is now an editor at *Futurepoem*, where he curates the blog *Futurepost*. After moving from Colorado to Minnesota to San Francisco, he currently resides in New York, where he teaches children and adults with learning differences.

Chris Martin recommends
these Coffee House Press books:

**Great Balls
of Fire**
by Ron Padgett

The Spoils
by Ted Mathys

Ripple Effect
by Elaine Equi

**Dancing on
Main Street**
by Lorenzo Thomas

**Notes on the
Possibilities
and Attractions
of Existence**
by Anselm Hollo

Darkacre
by Greg Hewett

The California Poem
by Eleni Sikelianos

**Nice to See You:
Homage to Ted
Berrigan**
edited by
Anne Waldman

COLOPHON

Becoming Weather was designed at Coffee House Press, in the historic
Grain Belt Brewery's Bottling House near downtown Minneapolis.
The text is set in Bembo.

FUNDER ACKNOWLEDGMENT

Coffee House Press is an independent nonprofit literary publisher. Our books are
made possible through the generous support of grants and gifts from many
foundations, corporate giving programs, state and federal support, and through
donations from individuals who believe in the transformational power of literature.
Coffee House Press receives major operating support from the Bush Foundation,
the Jerome Foundation, the McKnight Foundation, from Target, and from the
Minnesota State Arts Board, through an appropriation from the Minnesota State
Legislature and from the National Endowment for the Arts. Coffee House also
receives support from: three anonymous donors; Elmer L. and Eleanor J. Andersen
Foundation; Allan Appel; Around Town Literary Media Guides; Patricia Beithon;
Bill Berkson; the James L. and Nancy J. Bildner Foundation; the Patrick and Aimee
Butler Family Foundation; the Buuck Family Foundation; Dorsey & Whitney, LLP;
Fredrikson & Byron, P.A.; Sally French; Jennifer Haugh; Anselm Hollo and Jane
Dalrymple-Hollo; Jeffrey Hom; Stephen and Isabel Keating; the Kenneth Koch
Literary Estate; the Lenfestey Family Foundation; Ethan J. Litman; Mary
McDermid; Sjur Midness and Briar Andresen; the Rehael Fund of the Minneapolis
Foundation; Deborah Reynolds; Schwegman, Lundberg, Woessner, P.A.; John
Sjoberg; David Smith; Mary Strand and Tom Fraser; Jeffrey Sugerman; Patricia
Tilton; the Archie D. & Bertha H. Walker Foundation; Stu Wilson and Mel Barker;
the Woessner Freeman Family Foundation in memory of David Hilton; and many
other generous individual donors.

To you and our many readers across the country,
we send our thanks for your continuing support.

Good books are brewing at coffeehousepress.org